Wright Pocket Booster

OCR Gateway A
Physics 4, 5 and 6

For GCSE Combined Science Higher Tier

For my brother...who taught me resilience through annoying me endlessly as kids and whose photos I stole for some covers!

How to use this pocket booster

Each topic has a QR code at the end of the page. If you download a free QR code reader on your phone, this will then take you to the video about that topic on YouTube.

If you see a formula in a box – You need to learn it for the exam.

The key idea of this book is to carry it with you and just take those few minutes to read a couple of pages to check you know it. Learn it, revisit it and then review it again. The more you do this, the more information you will retain.

I hope that you find this book useful.

Subscribe to Wright Science on YouTube to for a full set of videos to support you in your GCSE science studies.

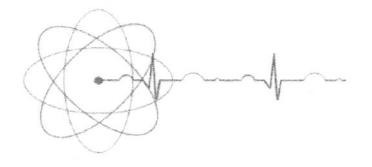

WRIGHT SCIENCE
SCIENCE DONE THE WRIGHT WAY

ISBN-13: 9781093601459

2019
© Vicki Wright

P4
Waves and Radioactivity

P4.1.1: Waves and their Properties

A wave is an oscillation that transfers energy.

There are two types of wave:
1. Mechanical waves (sound and water) need a medium to travel.
2. Electromagnetic waves do not need a medium to travel.

Waves can either be transverse or longitudinal.

In transverse waves, the vibrations are at 90° to the direction the wave travels.

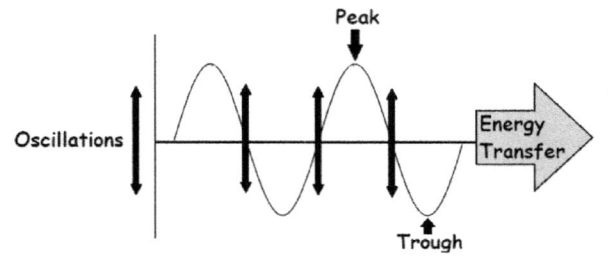

In longitudinal waves, the vibrations are in the same direction as the wave travels.

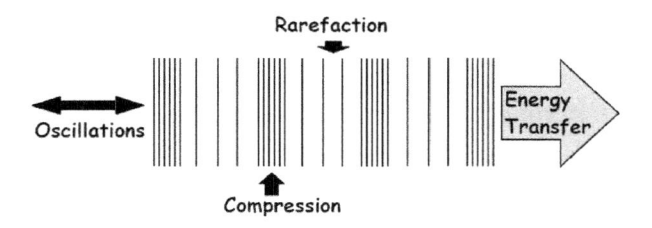

There are four wave properties we need to know:
1. Amplitude (A) – Distance from the middle to the top or bottom of the wave. Units depend on the wave.
2. Wavelength (λ) – Distance from one point on a wave to the same point on the next wave. Units are metres, m.
3. Frequency (F) – Number of waves or oscillations per second. Units are Hertz, Hz.
4. Time Period (T) – Time for one wave to pass a given point. Units are seconds, s.

Waves can be represented as either a time trace or a snapshot. Both graphs allow you to measure amplitude from the middle to the top or bottom of the wave.

A time trace shows how displacement varies with **time** at a position. We can measure the time period from any point on a wave to the same point on the next.

We can also calculate the time period using 1 ÷ Frequency

A snapshot shows how displacement varies with **distance** at a given time. It allows us to measure wavelength from any point on a wave to the same point on the next.

> *Exam hint: To identify if it is a time trace or snapshot, look at the x axis label.*

P4.1.2: Wave Velocity

Frequency: Number of waves passing a given point each second.

Wavelength: Distance from one point on a wave to the same point on the next wave.

> **Wave Velocity (m/s) = Frequency (Hz) x Wavelength (m)**

If we wanted to work out the velocity of a sound we can:
- Measure a distance you stand from a wall
- Clap and time how long it takes to hear an echo.
- Use speed = distance ÷ time

Alternatively, we can:
- Connect a pair of microphones a set distance apart to an oscilloscope

- Use the oscilloscope to work out the time between the wave reaching each microphone.
- Calculate the velocity.

The velocity of sound varies with:
- Temperature
- Pressure

Investigating Waves (PAG P4)

We use a ripple tank to investigate waves. To calculate the velocity of a wave, we need to know the wavelength and frequency.

To measure the wavelength either:
1. Place a ruler in the tank and measure the wavelength.
2. Use a stroboscope to 'freeze' the waves on a piece of paper on the desk below and then use a ruler to measure the wavelength.

To measure the frequency either:
1. Place a marker in the tank and count the waves passing it each second.
2. Place a small piece of paper touching the top of the vibrating bar as it vibrates. Listen to it and count the vibrations each second.

Do remember that in any technique that involves counting or measuring fast moving objects, humans may make errors.

A safety precaution with the stroboscope – Check for photosensitive people in your group.

Check Your Understanding

1. What are the two types of wave?

2. Draw a diagram to show transverse waves.

3. Draw a diagram to show a longitudinal wave.

4. What can be measured on a snap shot?

5. What is the formula for wave velocity?

6. Describe how to use a ripple tank to measure wave velocity.

P4.2.1: Electromagnetic Waves

When white light passes through a prism, you can see the visible light spectrum. Visible light is part of the electromagnetic spectrum.

The order of waves in the EM spectrum is:
- Radio waves
- Microwaves
- Infrared (IR)
- Visible light
- Ultraviolet (UV)
- X-Rays
- Gamma Rays

This shows the waves in increasing frequency and decreasing wavelength.

Electromagnetic waves consist of oscillating electric and magnetic fields. The fields oscillate at 90° to the direction of the wave.

All EM waves travel through a vacuum at 3.0×10^8 m/s. This is also the speed of light as it is part of the EM spectrum.

Sources emit EM waves e.g. microwave ovens emit microwaves. Objects also absorb EM waves e.g. skin absorbs infrared to heat up. EM waves transfer energy from sources to absorbers.

Radio waves are produced when an oscillating potential difference across a wire makes electrons move backwards and forwards. This produces a changing electric and magnetic field which is emitted as a radio wave.

Radio waves are detected as when the fields meet a piece of metal, the electrons move and an electrical signal is produced.

P4.2.2: EM Radiation Uses and Dangers

EM radiation is used in the following:
- Microwaves are used in mobile phones; satellites; Wi-Fi and Bluetooth.
- Radio waves are used in radio and TV.
- Infrared is used in remote controls and optical fibres.
- Visible light can be used to communicate between ships.
- Lasers in CDs, DVDs and Blu-rays use visible light to read the discs.
- X-rays can kill cancer cells and also produce images of bones.
- Gamma rays can kill bacteria and cancer cells.

Ultraviolet is useful for:
- The body producing vitamin D which you need for strong bones.
- Forensics officers identifying forged bank notes and find bodily fluids.
- Sterilising water by killing bacteria.

EM waves can also be used to transfer energy to cook food in two ways:

1. Microwave ovens emit microwaves which are absorbed by the fat and water in the food. They can penetrate a few centimetres into the food. The energy is then transferred by conduction to the middle.

2. Infrared radiation is absorbed by the particles on the surface of the food. The energy is then transferred by conduction to cook the rest of the food. Therefore, conventional ovens are slower at cooking food than microwaves.

Dangers

Ultraviolet can damage the DNA in skin cells leading to skin cancer. Too much exposure to UV light in your eyes can lead to cataracts.

X-rays can damage cells and cause cancer. Radiographers stand behind a lead screen or leave the room to reduce exposure. They also wear a badge that changes when the safe exposure limit has been reached.

Gamma rays can also kill or damage cells in the body.

Check Your Understanding

1. List the waves of the electromagnetic spectrum, starting with the longest wavelength.

2. What speed does ultraviolet travel at?

3. Explain how radio waves are produced.

4. Explain why microwaves cook food faster than infrared.

5. List two uses and two dangers of electromagnetic waves.

P4.3.1: Atoms and Isotopes

The nucleus of an atom is made up of protons and neutrons. The charge on the nucleus depends on the number of protons present. It is always positive.

Subatomic Particle	Relative Mass	Relative Charge
Proton	1	+1
Neutron	1	0
Electron	0.0005	-1

Isotope: Atom with the same atomic number but a different mass number because it has the same number of protons and electrons but a different number of neutrons. E.g. Carbon-12, Carbon-13 and Carbon-14

$$^{12}_{6}C \quad ^{13}_{6}C \quad ^{14}_{6}C$$

Each has 6 protons.
C-12 has 6 neutrons; C-13 has 7 neutrons and C-14 has 8 neutrons.

Atomic Number: Number of protons OR the number of electrons.

Mass Number: Number of protons + Number of neutrons

If asked to work out the number of protons or electrons in an atom, write down the atomic number from the periodic table.

If asked to work out the number of neutrons of an atom, subtract the atomic number from the mass number.

P4.3.2: Alpha, Beta and Gamma

Most atoms are stable – They do not decay. Atoms with an unstable nucleus will emit radiation as they decay. A material that emits radiation is radioactive.

There are four types of radiation:
1. Alpha particles (α) – Nucleus of a helium atom, ^4_2He.
2. Beta particles (β) – Fast moving electrons, $^{\ \ 0}_{-1}e$.
3. Gamma waves (γ) – Wave of the electromagnetic spectrum.
4. Neutron particles (n) – Particle in the nucleus, ^1_0n.

For the symbols, the top number is the mass relative to a proton and the bottom number is the charge.

The nucleus doesn't contain electrons, so the beta particle is formed from the decay of a neutron forming a proton and an electron.

If we need to detect radiation, we use a Geiger-Müller tube or Geiger counter. The clicks that are heard are tiny currents produced when the radiation ionises atoms of the gas inside the tube.

Radiation emitted by radioactive material is ionising radiation. Ionising radiation can remove electrons from atoms to produce positively charged ions. To ionise an atom, energy must be transferred to it. Alpha particles transfer more energy to the material they travel through hence, their short range.

Alpha, beta and gamma have different penetrating powers.

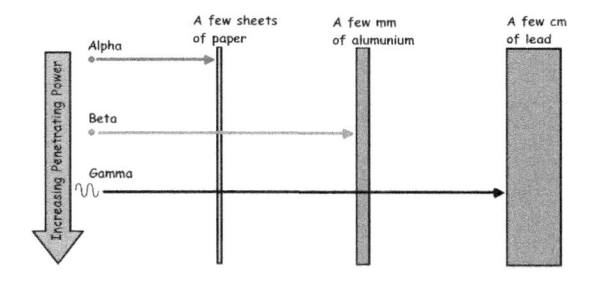

Increasing Penetrating Power

Alpha → A few sheets of paper

Beta → A few mm of alumunium

Gamma → A few cm of lead

Key Properties of Radiations

Alpha
Relative mass: Large
Charge: +2
Ionising Power: High
Range: Short

Beta
Relative mass: Small
Charge: -1
Ionising Power: Medium
Range: Medium

Gamma
Relative mass: None
Charge: None
Ionising Power: Low
Range: Long

P4.3.3: Nuclear Equations

Alpha Decay

An alpha particle is emitted which is made of two protons and two neutrons (helium nucleus).

$$^{240}_{94}Pu \rightarrow \,^{236}_{92}U + \,^{4}_{2}He$$

The mass decreases by 4 and the atomic number decreases by 2 so a new element is formed.

Beta Decay

A neutron decays to a proton and an electron.

$$^{14}_{6}C \rightarrow \,^{14}_{7}N + \,^{0}_{-1}e$$

The mass does not change as the total number of protons and neutrons remains the same (1 neutron is lost but 1 proton is gained). The atomic number increases by 1 so a new element is formed.

Gamma Decay

Gamma rays are electromagnetic waves and have no mass or charge. This means there is no change in the mass number or atomic number.

Neutron Emission

The decay of some nuclei leads to the production of large numbers of neutrons. These neutrons are then emitted to make it stable.

E.g. helium-5

$$^5_2He \rightarrow {}^4_2He + {}^1_0n$$

> *Exam hint: If you know the symbols for the types of radiation, you can work out whatever else is missing from the question.*

P6.3.4: Half-Life

Radiation is emitted at random. A Geiger counter can be used to measure the radiation. This measures the activity. Activity (Count): Radiation emitted per second. Measured in Becquerels (Bq).

Half-Life: Time it takes for the activity to halve. It is also the time is takes for half the unstable nuclei to decay. The half-life of a material may be long or short.

There are two ways to calculate half-life.
1. Using calculations:
E.g. A sample of radon-222 has an activity of 100Bq. Calculate the activity after 11.4 days. The half-life of radon-222 is 3.8 days.
Step 1: Calculate the number of half-lives.
11.4 ÷ 3.8 = 3 half-lives
Step 2: Calculate the new activity.
($\frac{1}{2} \times \frac{1}{2} \times \frac{1}{2}$) × 100 = 12.5Bq

2. From a graph:
- Look at the total activity on time 0.
- Divide it by 2.
- Draw a horizontal line across from this number to the curve.
- Where the line meets the curve, draw a vertical line to the time axis and read off the value.

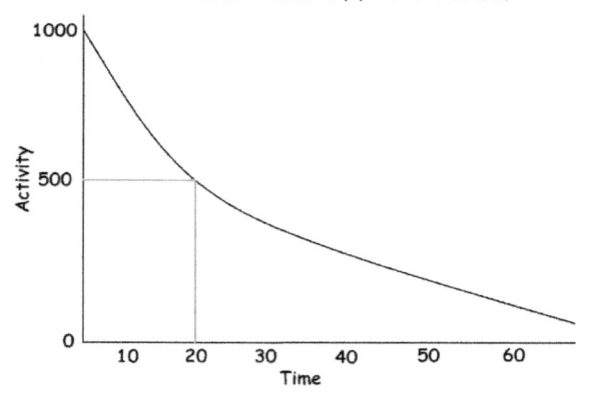

P4.3.5: Radiation in and out of Atoms

Electrons occupy certain energy levels around the nucleus. Different atoms have different energy levels. Electrons usually occupy the lowest possible energy level (the smallest distance from the nucleus).

In the photon model, electromagnetic radiation is emitted and absorbed as packets of energy called photons. The energy of each photon is proportional to the frequency. In order to excite an electron to a higher energy level, a photon of the right energy must be absorbed. Once the photon has been absorbed, the electron moves to the higher energy level and the atom is in an excited state.

If light of all frequencies is passed through hydrogen gas, some frequencies are absorbed and an absorption spectrum is produced which shows a set of frequencies of radiation absorbed by an atom when excited electrons move to higher energy levels. The black lines are the frequencies absorbed.

A photon that has enough energy can completely remove an electron from the atom. This atom is ionised. Photons of UV, X-ray and gamma ray frequencies have enough energy to ionise atoms.

When electrons move from a higher to lower energy level, they emit radiation. An emission spectrum shows a set of frequencies of radiation emitted by an atom when excited electrons move to a lower energy level. The frequency of radiation emitted depends on the difference in energy of the energy levels.

This energy change can take place in one go or two or more. If it occurs over two or more, then the emitted photons will have less energy, lower frequencies and longer wavelengths.

The largest energy difference is from an energy level just below ionisation. This will vary in different atoms:
E.g.
Hydrogen can emit UV photons
But
Carbon can emit X-ray photons.

Protons and neutrons occupy energy levels in the nucleus and can emit gamma rays as the energy involved is much higher.

P4.3.6: Radiation and the Human Body

Background radiation is made up of sources of radiation that we are exposed to all the time. Background radiation comes from:
- Radon gas 50.0%
- Medical uses 14.0%
- Ground and buildings 14.0%
- Food and drink 11.5%
- Cosmic rays 10.0%
- Other 0.2%
- Nuclear weapon tests 0.2%
- Nuclear power 0.1%

Contamination – Occurs when radioactive material is taken inside the body or on the skin. Internal contamination cannot be removed.

Irradiation – Occurs when radioactive material is outside your body. The radiation can travel into the body.

The problem of radiation is that when it enters the body, the DNA inside the cells can be damaged and this can lead to cancer. Radioactive materials are a hazard but the risk of cancer as a result of exposure to low doses is very low. Small doses of radiation lead to damage that can be repaired by the body.

Check Your Understanding

1. What is the relative mass and relative charge on each subatomic particle?

2. Define the term isotope.

3. Describe the four types of radiation.

4. Compare the penetrating and ionising powers of alpha, beta and gamma radiation.

5. Describe the four types of decay, including the equations.

6. Define the term half-life.

7. Explain how to calculate half-life.

8. Describe how an absorption spectrum is formed.

P5 Energy

P5.1.1: Energy Stores and Energy Transfers

Energy is a quantity in joules (J) that tells you what is possible but does not tell you what will happen.

There are 8 energy stores you need to remember and their related formulae:

1. Chemical store e.g. glucose in your muscles or a fuel with oxygen.

2. Thermal store e.g. a hot bath
Energy (J) =
Mass (kg) × SHC (J/kg°C) × Temperature Change (°C)

3. Kinetic store e.g. moving car

> **Energy (J) =
> 0.5 × Mass (kg) × Speed^2 (m/s)**

4. Gravitational store e.g. diver standing on a diving board

> **Energy (J) = Mass (kg) x g (N/kg) x Height (m)**

5. Elastic store e.g. stretched elastic band
Energy (J) = 0.5 x Spring Constant (N/m) x Extension^2 (m)

6. Nuclear store e.g. Uranium-235
Energy (J) = Change in Mass (kg) x Speed of light^2 (m/s)

7. Electrostatic store e.g. two opposite charges held apart

8. Magnetic store e.g. two opposite poles of a magnet held apart

There are four ways that energy is transferred between the stores:
1. Mechanically
2. Electrically
3. Heating by particles
4. Heating by radiation

We can calculate the energy transferred mechanically using the formula:

Work Done (J) = Force (N) x Distance (m)

We can calculate the energy transferred electrically using the formula:

Energy Transfer (J) = Power (W) x Time (s)

Energy cannot be created or destroyed. It can only be transferred between stores. This is the law of conservation of energy. Closed systems will have no net energy change.

P5.1.2: Energy Analysis with Forces 1

To carry out an energy analysis you need to:
- Choose 2 points in a process
- Identify which stores have more or less energy in them at those points.
- Work out which type of transfer has occurred between the stores.

Example: A racing car
At the start of the race:
Stationary car - Kinetic store is empty
There is lots of fuel and oxygen - Chemical store has lots of energy

At the end of the race:
Moving car - Kinetic store has some energy
There is less fuel and oxygen - Chemical store has less energy

Transfer:
Engine exerting a force - Mechanically

We can represent this on an energy analysis diagram.

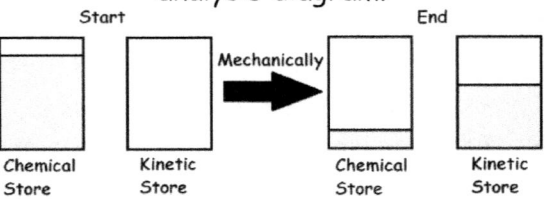

Start → Mechanically → End

Chemical Store | Kinetic Store | Chemical Store | Kinetic Store

In a closed system, the decrease in energy in the chemical store is equal to the increase in the kinetic store due to the mechanical work done.

In reality, not all energy is transferred to kinetic energy. Some energy is transferred to the thermal store due to friction, sound or air resistance.

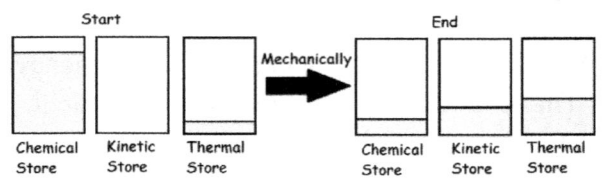

Start → Mechanically → End

Chemical Store | Kinetic Store | Thermal Store | Chemical Store | Kinetic Store | Thermal Store

You may be asked to use the formulae you have learnt over the physics course to calculate energy changes.

E.g. A drag racer, starting from rest, exerts a force of 4000N over 300m. Calculate the work done. The mass of the racer is 300kg, calculate the final speed.

Step 1: Identify the formula to use
Work Done = Force x Distance

Step 2: Substitute in and solve
Work Done = 4000 x 300 =1,200,000J

Step 3: Identify the next formula to use.
Kinetic Energy = 0.5 x Mass x Speed^2

Step 4: Rearrange, substitute in and solve.
Speed = $\sqrt{(2E \div m)}$
= $\sqrt{(2 \times 1,200,000 \div 300)}$ = 90m/s

P5.1.3: Energy Analysis with Forces 2

Brakes exert a force on a car which results in energy being transferred from the kinetic store to the thermal store.

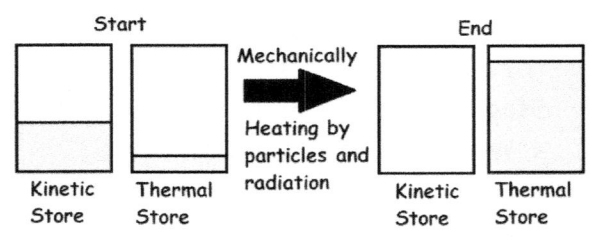

Start — Kinetic Store, Thermal Store

Mechanically

Heating by particles and radiation

End — Kinetic Store, Thermal Store

Here the car is moving initially and the surroundings are cool so there is some energy in the kinetic store and thermal store. After the brakes have been applied, the car stops and the brakes heat up due to friction.

A gymnast jumping on a springboard would have an energy analysis as follows:

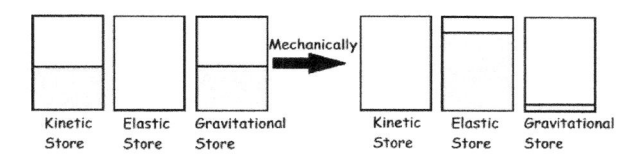

| Kinetic Store | Elastic Store | Gravitational Store | Mechanically → | Kinetic Store | Elastic Store | Gravitational Store |

At the start the gymnast is in the air above the springboard so the elastic store is empty, kinetic store has energy and the gravitational store has energy. At the end, the springboard is compressed and the gymnast has a moment where they are stationary. So the elastic store has energy, gravitational store has a little energy and the kinetic store is empty.

> *Exam hint: Look at the question to work out what stores are involved to select the right formula for calculations.*

P5.1.4: Energy Analysis with Forces 3

If you imagine a situation where you throw a ball up in the air:
Initially the ball is moving up and is quite close to the Earth so there is some GPE and some kinetic energy. When the ball reaches its peak it comes to a momentary stop so has no kinetic energy and lots of GPE as it is high off the ground.

The energy analysis diagram would look like this:

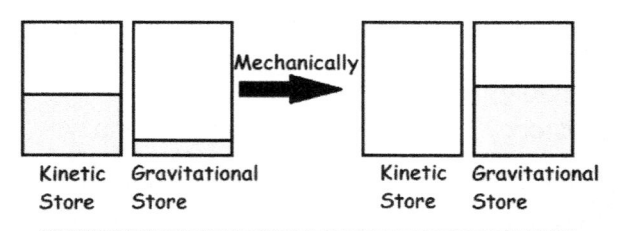

| Kinetic Store | Gravitational Store | Mechanically → | Kinetic Store | Gravitational Store |

Exam hint: Remember acceleration due to gravity is 10m/s^2.

Remember that because some energy is transferred to the thermal store by friction, the ball will not reach the maximum height possible. Our energy analysis diagram should include a thermal store too.

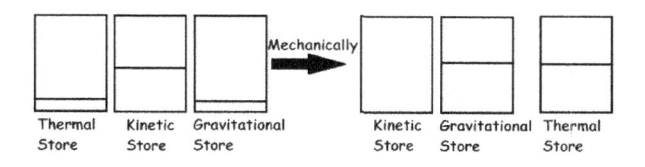

| Thermal Store | Kinetic Store | Gravitational Store | →Mechanically | Kinetic Store | Gravitational Store | Thermal Store |

Check Your Understanding

1. List the 8 energy stores.

2. List the 4 energy transfers.

3. What formula would you use to calculate kinetic energy?

4. What formula would you use to calculate gravitational potential energy?

5. Draw an energy analysis diagram for a car in a drag race.

6. A drag racer comes to a stop over 50m. Calculate the force exerted by the brakes. The energy in the kinetic store before braking is 1.2×10^6 J.

P5.2.1: Energy, Power and Paying for Electricity

Energy is transferred when charge moves from a battery or power station.

The energy store in a battery is a chemical store.

The energy store in a power plant is either a chemical store or a nuclear store, depending on the type of power plant.

Electrons in the wire produce light, a heating effect or make a motor turn to transfer energy.

Electrical devices have a power rating in watts (W) or kilowatts (kW).

Power: The rate of transfer of energy or the work done/time.

In our homes, the energy transferred by electrical appliances is measured with an electricity meter.

The meters use the kilowatt-hour as the unit of energy. A unit is the energy transferred by a 1kW appliance when it is on for 1 hour.

Work Done (kWh) = Power (kW) x Time (h)

Power (W) = Work Done (J) ÷ Time (s)

Exam hint: If you are asked to calculate the cost of running an appliance then work out the units used first and then multiply this by the cost per unit.

P5.2.2: Energy Analysis – Electric Current

An electrical appliance transfers energy from chemical stores to other stores electrically.

E.g.

Hairdryers dry your hair by using the energy:
- Transferred electrically to produce heating by radiation
- Transferred mechanically to move the fan and air

If the device being used has a higher power rating, the amount of fuel it needs to run it is greater than that needed for a lower power device.

This means it will carry out jobs faster but uses more fuel to do it.

When current flows in a wire, the wire heats up. This means energy is transferred to a thermal store when you use an electrical appliance. This energy is wasted.

> *Exam hint: Remember that if you are asked to calculate energy changes when heating water, you will need the specific heat capacity formula from the data sheet.*

P5.2.3: Energy Analysis - Heating

Energy in a thermal store is increased by heating, usually by:
- Burning a fuel
- Using electric current to transfer energy from a fuel

If a temperature difference exists between two objects, energy transfer occurs. The hot object (source) transfers energy to the colder object (sink) until they are at equilibrium. The rate of transfer is faster when the temperature difference is greater.

Storage heaters contain concrete which heats up when the heating is on and then releases the stored energy through the day when the heating is off. This can be a cost-effective way of heating if you have an energy plan that costs less overnight.

Dissipation: The transfer of energy to stores that are not useful which cannot be used for working or heating.

E.g. friction between moving parts leads to those parts heating up.

Ultimately, energy will end up in the thermal store of the surroundings.

Dissipation can be reduced by:
- Lubricating items – Reduces dissipation by friction by placing a layer of fluid between two solid surfaces which prevents direct contact.
- Insulating items – Reduces dissipation by heating by placing a poor conductor between a hot object and a cold one which reduces the rate of energy transfer.

P5.2.4: Walls and Insulation

When it is cold, we use the heating in our homes to keep them warm. If the heating is turned off, the house cools down as energy is transferred to the surroundings via windows, walls etc.

The rate at which energy is transferred through the walls depends upon their thickness, the material they are made of and the temperature difference between inside and outside.

Most houses there are two layers of stone or brick with insulation between. This is a cavity wall.

Cavity filled with insulation

External Wall — Internal Wall

Thermal conductivity of a material tells you the rate at which it transfers energy though a wall with:
- An area of 1m^2
- A thickness of 1m
- A temperature difference of 1^{O}C

The higher the thermal conductivity, the faster the material transfers energy and therefore leads to faster cooling.

To reduce the rate of cooling:
- Have thicker walls
- How lower thermal conductivity of the materials used to make them or insulate them

P5.2.5: Efficiency

An efficient device is better at transferring energy between stores that do the job we want.

Efficiency = (Useful Output Energy ÷ Input Energy) x 100

Exam hint: Think about the intended use of the object to identify which energy type is useful and which is wasted.

E.g. A lamp has an input of 100J. The output to light is 60J and the output to heat is 40J. Calculate the efficiency of the light bulb.

Useful Energy = Light = 60J
Wasted Energy = Heat = 40J
Efficiency = (60 ÷ 100) x 100
=60%

Sankey diagrams are used to show the efficiency. The width of the arrow shows the amount of energy transferred.

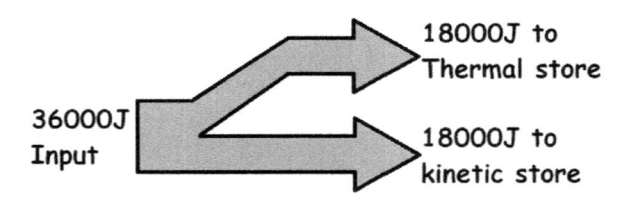

36000J Input → 18000J to Thermal store / 18000J to kinetic store

To increase efficiency, you must reduce the wasted energy.
This can be achieved by:
- Insulating
- Using materials that reduce unwanted energy transfer
- Use improved technology e.g. LED

More efficient devices operate at a lower power so use fuels more slowly.

Check Your Understanding

1. What does the power rating tell us?

2. What is the formula for calculating the work done by an appliance?

3. Explain the energy transfers in a hairdryer

4. Define the term dissipation.

5. Explain how you can reduce the amount of energy dissipated in an object.

6. Explain how to reduce the energy transfers from your home to the surroundings.

7. How do you calculate efficiency?

8. How can you increase efficiency?

P6 Global Challenges

P6.1.1: Speed

There are a range of instruments we use to measure speed in our everyday lives. These include speed cameras, speed guns, electronic timers and satnav systems.

If you consider how the distance is measured, it may be using a tape measure, trundle wheel or by comparing the distance to different satellites.

To work out the time we may use an electronic timer, the time between two photos or pressure sensors to start a timer and a laser being broken to end it.

> **Speed (m/s) = Distance (m) ÷ Time (s)**

You need to know some typical speeds of objects in everyday situations. Here is a selection:
- A person walking = 1m/s (2.2mph)

- A person running = 5m/s (11mph)
  - A cyclist = 7m/s (15mph)
  - A car = 22m/s (50mph)
- Sound = 330m/s (738mph)

> *Exam hint: Make sure you know at least one fast and one slow object. You can then estimate others.*

You may also be asked to use the acceleration formula in everyday situations.

Acceleration (m/s^2) = Change in Speed (m/s) ÷ Time (s)

When talking about data, we may see these terms used:

Precise: Data has a small range when repeated.

Accurate: Close to the true value.

P6.1.2: Reaction Time and Thinking Distance

Reaction Time = Time taken from seeing something to the reaction (putting on the brake or pressing the stopwatch button).

Human reaction time is about 0.2 seconds.

Reaction times can be measured by dropping a ruler and catching it or by using a reaction time tester on the computer.

Thinking Distance = Distance travelled in the time it takes from seeing a potential problem to starting to apply the brakes.

> *Exam hint: Don't forget it is a DISTANCE so it is how far you travel in the time it takes to react.*

Thinking distance will be increased by:
- Drinking alcohol
- Using drugs
- Being tired
- Distractions
- Eating or drinking
- Using a sat nav or radio or mobile phone
- Increased speed

Exam hint: Thinking distance is anything that impacts on the person and their ability to react.

Exam hint: Drugs and alcohol usually are classed as the same marking point so only use one of those.

P6.1.3: Braking Distance and Stopping Distance

Braking Distance = Distance travelled in the time it takes from putting the foot on the brake to coming to a stop.

> *Exam hint: Don't forget it is a DISTANCE so it is how far you travel in the time it takes to stop.*

Factors that increase the braking distance:
- Increased speed
- Icy or wet roads
- Poor brake condition
- Poor tyre condition

> *Exam hint: Braking distance is about a factor that impacts on the car*

Stopping Distance = Total distance travelled from the moment the driver sees the problem to coming to a stop.

Stopping Distance = Thinking Distance + Braking Distance

If we consider how speed affects the thinking and braking distance, they both increase with increased speed. However, thinking distance increases in a linear fashion.

E.g. 20mph = 6m
30mph = 9m
40mph = 12m

It increases by 3m for every 10mph.

Speed	Thinking	Braking	Stopping
20mph	6	6	12
30mph	9	14	23
40mph	12	24	36
50mph	15	38	53
60mph	18	55	73
70mph	21	75	96

P6.1.4: Forces in Collisions

When wearing a seatbelt and the car comes to a sudden stop, you move forward and the seatbelt stretches and brings you to a slower stop. This reduces the forces acting on your body. Seatbelts need replacing after a crash as they have been stretched.

When not wearing a seatbelt and the car comes to a sudden stop, you continue to move forwards at the original speed until something stops you.

If the negative acceleration is very large, you can suffer compression injuries from the seatbelt or the internal organs can be damaged as they collide with the ribs.

Check Your Understanding

1. How would you measure the distance in a 100m race?

2. How would you measure the time in a speed camera?

3. What is the typical speed of a person walking?

4. What is the typical speed of a person running?

5. List three factors that increase thinking distance.

6. List three factors that increase braking distance.

7. Explain why you should wear a seatbelt in cars.

P6.2.1: Energy Sources

An energy source is something we can use for heating, transportation or generating electricity.

Energy sources are either renewable or non-renewable.

Renewable: Will not run out.

Non-Renewable: Will run out. Being used faster than it is being made.

Renewable energy sources:
- Biofuels
- Solar
- Tides
- Wind
- Waves
- Geothermal
- Hydroelectric

Non-renewable energy sources:
- Fossil Fuels – Coal, oil and natural gas
- Nuclear fuels

Nuclear fuels were formed in stars.

Fossil fuels were formed from the effects of pressure and temperature on the remains of living things over millions of years.

There are three main uses of energy sources:
1. Heating E.g. fossil fuels; biofuels, Sun and geothermal
2. Transportation E.g. Fossil fuels and biofuels
3. Generating Electricity

We can also heat our houses by:
- Building houses that maximise heat from the sun.
- Use solar panels
- Use hot water from underground (in some areas)

We can generate electricity by:
- Using photovoltaic cells (solar cells)
- Use turbines and generators driven by wind, waves, geothermal, hydroelectric or biofuels.

P6.2.2: Using Resources

The use of energy sources over time has changed because there has been an increase in population, our use of devices has changed, and we use more electricity. This results in increased electricity generation and increased use of devices that use fuels.

The supply of fossil fuels is finite – They will run out.

There are reserves of fossil fuels in many parts of the world that are hard to reach. The harder fossil fuels are to find and extract, the more expensive they become.

Burning fossil fuels produces the gas carbon dioxide. This leads to climate change and the greenhouse effect.

Climate change leads to:
- Ice caps melting
- Sea levels rise
- Flooding
- Extreme weather events
- Threats to food supplies

When a government decides what energy source to use, they need to consider:
- Cost
- Environmental impact
- How long the sources will last

P6.2.3: The National Grid

The National Grid is the system of cables, power stations, transformers and sub-stations that transport electricity across the country.

Transformers change the voltage (p.d.) to reduce the heating effect.

Step-Up transformers: Increase the p.d. or voltage.

Step-Down transformers: Decrease the p.d. or voltage.

If the wires heat up, energy is lost to the surroundings. The amount of heating depends on current and resistance.

P6.2.4: Mains Electricity

Mains electricity has a voltage of 230V. Generators in power stations create an alternating voltage with a frequency of 50Hz. This reaches our houses through the National Grid.

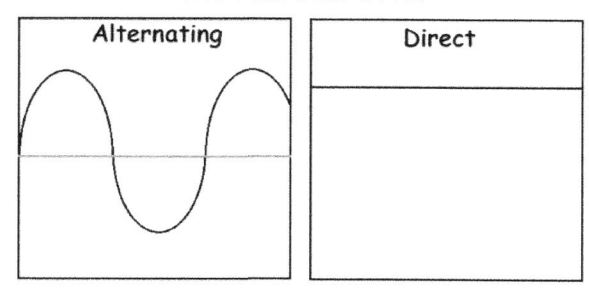

Alternating	Direct
(sine wave)	(flat line)

Batteries create a direct voltage.

In the UK, our plugs have three wires inside. The live (brown) and neutral (blue) wire make a complete circuit with the appliance. The earth (yellow and green) wire is connected to earth.

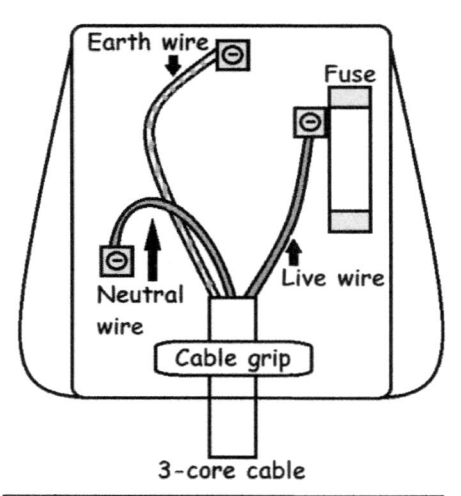

Voltmeter between	Potential Difference
Live and Neutral	230V
Live and Earth	230V
Neutral and Earth	0V

We have a few key safety features inside our plugs to reduce the risk of electrocution.

If the live wire comes loose and touches the metal case on an appliance, it becomes live and you could be electrocuted. The earth wire connects to the case and the earth pole so the current flows into the earth wire and not you as it has less resistance than you do. The fuse will also melt to break the circuit and stop the current flowing.

Double insulated appliances: Case is plastic so no current can flow through the case to you. These do not need an earth.

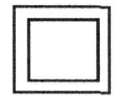

Check Your Understanding

1. Explain the difference between renewable and non-renewable.

2. Give two examples of renewable energy sources.

3. Give two examples of non-renewable energy sources.

4. Explain why our use of energy sources has changed over the past 150 years.

5. Explain the problems of burning fossil fuels.

6. Explain how electricity is transmitted from the power station to our home.

7. Describe how a UK plug is wired.

About Wright Science

Wright Science is a YouTube channel created by Vicki Wright, a secondary science teacher in England.

I started Wright Science as a resource for my own classes to have extra help outside of school time. It started with a single recap video for each exam back in 2013 and then just grew. These days there are videos for every lesson on both the separate science courses and combined science courses which are used by a number of students across the country and world!

I hope that you find this book useful and welcome your comments.

Good luck in your exams!

Printed in Great Britain
by Amazon